# POETIC EMOTIONS OF A BEAUTIFUL YOUNG SOUL

100 POEMS OF LIFE, LOVE, PAIN & HOPE

By L. Marcia Williams

All rights reserved. No portion of this book may be reproduced, stored in a retrieval system, or transmitted in any form or by any means – electronic, mechanical, photocopy, recording, scanning, or other – except for brief quotations in critical reviews or articles without the prior written permission of the publisher.

Published in Valrico, Florida by:
Willaw Publishing
P.O. Box 6295
Brandon, FL 33508
Email address: willawpublishing@gmail.com

Book cover layout and design created by freelance designer, Michael Akins (info@michaelakins.com) in Clearwater, Florida. Photography work done by freelance photographer, Nikeya Williams of NSW Photography (nikeyaw07@gmail.com), Tampa, Florida. Edited by L. Marcia Williams and Charmaine Oliver, Tampa, Florida. Additional editing by Angela Judge, Tampa, Florida. Page layout and design by Angie "A. Euseary" Marie of iamART Graphic Arts (infomysteryous@gmail.com), Tampa, Florida.

Copyright ©2013 by LaWanda Marcia Williams

All rights reserved.

Printed in the United States of America.

ISBN: 978-0-615-78746-6
August 2013

## Dedication

I dedicate this book to my mother, Claty Williams, who has always encouraged me, believed in me, and taught me that "I can do all things through Christ which strengtheneth me."

To my Aunt Gwendolyn Lorraine Muse: words can't explain how much I love and miss you. As a writer, you saw the gift in me and encouraged me every step of the way. I remember the wonderful times when we read our poems to each other and will forever cherish those memories. You were an angel who now has her wings.

## Acknowledgments

I would first like to say thank you to my Lord and Savior Jesus Christ for giving me the words to write each poem in this book. I appreciate the opportunity to share this gift that is a blessing from God with others.

I would like to acknowledge and thank my mother, Claty Williams, and my siblings Carla, LaToya and Searum for encouraging me and always being there for me.

To my nieces Kentreia, Mi'chael, Mica, Tiffany, and Jessica and to my nephew Marcus: I love you and know that God has great plans for each of your lives.

To my Grandmother, Annie Mary Hicks: I love you so much! Thank you for all of the lessons that you instilled in me at an early age. I will never forget them.

To my Aunt Adriane: thanks for always encouraging me and telling me that God had a plan for my life.

To the rest of my aunts, uncles and cousins: thanks for your love and support.

To my friends Nikeya, Angela, Mike, Charmaine, and the Rhone family: thank you for your support and encouragement. It means a lot.

To my dad, Willie Williams: thank you for providing for me. May God bless you and give you peace.

I would also like to give special thanks to Michael Akins, Angela Euseary, Charmaine Oliver and Nikeya Williams for your work on this project.

## Table of Contents

INTRODUCTION ................................................................. 1

LIFE ................................................................................... 3
    ALMOST GONE ............................................................ 5
    ANTI-BULLY .................................................................. 6
    ANTI-DRUG ................................................................... 7
    ASSUMPTIONS ............................................................. 8
    ATTITUDE ..................................................................... 9
    BEAUTIFUL COLORS .................................................10
    CHOCOLATE BAR ......................................................11
    DARKNESS EXPOSED ...............................................12
    DEAD WEIGHT ...........................................................13
    EXPOSÉ ........................................................................15
    FINAL NOTICE ............................................................16
    FRENEMY ....................................................................18
    IN MY OWN SKIN .....................................................19
    L-I-F-E ...........................................................................21
    LIFE'S BLINDSIDES ...................................................23
    LIFE'S WARS ...............................................................24
    MISUNDERSTOOD ....................................................25
    NOT YOUR FAULT .....................................................26
    PURITY .........................................................................27
    S-E-X ( THE 2ND REVELATION) ............................28

*Table of Contents*

| | |
|---|---|
| SEPTEMBER 11 | 30 |
| SKIN TONE | 31 |
| TOMORROW | 32 |
| VICE | 34 |
| WORTH | 36 |

**LOVE** ............ 39

| | |
|---|---|
| 5 AM ALARM | 41 |
| ALMOST LOVE | 42 |
| ASSURED LOVE | 43 |
| BEST FRIEND | 44 |
| CATCHING FEELINGS | 45 |
| ENCOMPASSED BY LOVE | 46 |
| FOREVER ENDLESSLY | 47 |
| GUIDED BY LOVE | 48 |
| I LOVE YOU | 49 |
| I WANT TO KNOW | 50 |
| LOVE | 51 |
| LOVE AT WAR | 52 |
| LOVE DRUG | 53 |
| LOVE INTEREST | 54 |
| LOVE UNAFRAID | 56 |
| LOVE UNFAMILIAR | 57 |
| LOVELY FEELINGS | 58 |
| ROUND AND ROUND GAME | 59 |
| STUNNER (BOY MEETS GIRL) | 60 |
| THE WAY | 61 |
| THE WAYS THAT I LOVE YOU | 62 |
| WHEN I LOOKED INTO YOUR EYES | 63 |
| YOU NEVER KNEW | 64 |

*Table of Contents*

YOUNG LOVE ............................................................. 65
YOUR LOVE .............................................................. 66

# PAIN ........................................................................ 69
4-GET ME NOT ......................................................... 71
ALONE ..................................................................... 72
BETRAYAL ............................................................... 73
DESPISE .................................................................. 74
DIGESTING PAIN ..................................................... 75
HANGING HOPES ................................................... 76
HARSH REALITIES .................................................. 77
HEART SCARS ........................................................ 78
HIGH SCHOOL PAIN ............................................... 79
HOSTAGE ................................................................ 81
JEKYLL AND HYDE .................................................. 82
LOVE DISINTEGRATED ........................................... 83
MY DEAR SWEET AUNT (GWEN MUSE) ................ 84
MY PEN, PAD AND I ............................................... 85
NIGHT CRIMES ....................................................... 86
NIGHTMARE ON MY STREET ................................. 87
ONE SHOT .............................................................. 89
PAIN EXTREME ....................................................... 90
PAINFUL LESSONS .................................................. 92
PAINFULLY EXISTING .............................................. 93
STOLEN INNOCENCE ............................................. 94
THE BATTLE INSIDE ................................................ 95
WALKING AWAY FROM PAIN ................................. 96
YOU KNOW WHAT! ................................................ 97
YOU SAID THAT YOU LOVED ME ........................... 98

## Table of Contents

HOPE ............................................................................ 101
   A FRIEND .................................................................. 103
   BEAUTY .................................................................... 104
   BEHIND CLOSED EYELIDS ..................................... 105
   BFF'S ......................................................................... 106
   BRIGHT FUTURE ..................................................... 107
   CHANGED WAYS ..................................................... 108
   GLUE ......................................................................... 109
   HERSTORY ............................................................... 110
   HOPE FOR A NATION .............................................. 111
   HOPEFUL DESIRE .................................................... 112
   HOPELESSNESS (DON'T GIVE IN) ........................... 113
   IT'S NOT OVER! ....................................................... 114
   KING .......................................................................... 115
   MY HOPE FOR YOU ................................................. 116
   MY ONE HOPE ......................................................... 118
   OVER-EXPOSED ....................................................... 119
   OVERCOMING CHALLENGES .................................. 120
   RIDE OR DIE ............................................................. 121
   THANK YOU .............................................................. 122
   THE BEAUTY OF YOUR SOUL ................................. 123
   THE GIFT OF TRUE FRIENDSHIP ............................ 124
   THOUSANDS OF TEARS .......................................... 125
   UNCERTAINTY ......................................................... 126
   UNDISGUISED .......................................................... 127
   WITH MY EYES OPEN WIDE ................................... 128

ABOUT THE AUTHOR .................................................... 131

# Introduction

Poetic Emotions of a Beautiful Young Soul is a collection of poems that deals with the topics of Life, Love, Pain & Hope.

As people, we attempt to cope with life through our loves, laughter and tears, hoping that we'll be better in the end for it.

This collection of poems illustrates the strong emotions we, as young people, may feel as we try to navigate the roads of Life through Love, Pain and Hope.

# LIFE

## Almost Gone

I feel like I'm almost gone,
And I can't get back, because I've gone too far,
Far away from what I've been taught,
So far away that I feel like a lost cause.

I've gotten into things I shouldn't have,
Followed a road that led to a destructive path,
And now I'm left with a mess to deal with.

I'm so ashamed that I often plead the fifth
When asked about what I'm going through.
Afraid of the rejection and scorn,
If only they knew the truth.

But something inside
Is telling me not to give up hope,
That I can get through this,
That there's a way to cope.

By talking through my problems
And pouring out my heart
To someone who's been here
Who knows I'm not almost gone.

## Anti-Bully

I live the life of an anti-bully:
One who accepts those for who they are whether or not I agree.

I live the life of an anti-bully:
I never put down others because they're different from me.

I live the life of an anti-bully:
I seek to spread love and generate peace.

I live the life of an anti-bully:
I'm on a mission to kill violence and make hatred cease.

I live the life of an anti-bully:
Because in this day and time, this is what we need.

I live the life of an anti-bully:
So why don't you join me and put an end to bullying?

## Anti-Drug

I choose to be an anti-drug in my community.
In my presence, you'll feel nothing but unity
And clear thoughts that won't cloud your judgment.

You won't lose yourself or have negative side effects.
I get high off life through working hard to reach goals,
Instead of needles and pills that kill your body and soul.

If you search, you'll find more anti-drugs like me.
Just look a little closer; we're not an anomaly.

We have everything that ordinary drugs don't have,
Like bright futures and endless possibilities in our paths.

So choose to be an anti-drug in your community.
Be an influence on others and make changes socially.

## Assumptions

The joke was on me when I assumed that you loved me.
But over space and time you sure enough showed me
That I wasn't worth much to you.
And maybe deep down I knew the truth,
When your winks were persistent for other girls around you.
When you didn't return my calls or texts
But always had a ready excuse.
I guess the question should be, 'How could I ever assume
That you loved Me?' when your actions proved
You couldn't, and I stayed when I shouldn't.
But I'm no longer under the false assumption
That your heart feels something that it doesn't.
Now, my heart is finally being set free by me,
Who is facing reality.

## Attitude

I don't understand
how you try to figure me.
You know I'm not as bad
as I may appear to be.

You seem to think that
I have a really bad attitude.
But I just want to let you know
that I really don't mean to come off as rude.

You say that I seem
to take correction as an attack.
Well maybe it's because
I've been attacked so much
that is the only way I know to react.

## Beautiful Colors

When I look out my window
I see an array of beautiful colors,

Colors that blend in harmony
to compliment one another.

They come in different shades
but are the same on the inside.

No color is superior;
They have equal value in life.

We all should have this outlook
when viewing members of society,

For it is the way the Creator
intended for things to be.

## Chocolate Bar

My skin is the color of a chocolate bar,
yet you're frightened when you see me.

How could the color of something so sweet
make you react so negatively?

It saddens me that I am judged by my outer being,
instead of what's on the inside of me.

And what's on the inside is love
and intelligence of a citizen that is law abiding.

I walk uprightly, but instead you see a thug,
dealer or gangster through veiled eyes.

But the content of one's character has nothing to do
with the color of their skin is what you fail to realize.

So, when you see me out and about
in skin that reminds you of that oh so sweet chocolate bar,

Give me the benefit of the doubt that I'm just as sweet
on the inside as the world's finest chocolate bar.

## Darkness Exposed

You exposed the very darkness of my soul.
I thought others couldn't see it through the blindfold

I'd placed over their eyes, so they wouldn't realize
The type of demons I unsuccessfully battled inside.

But they were all brought to the forefront that fateful day
You shed light on all my hidden parts, put them on display.

No longer could I do dirt in the corner and in the dark.
This was you pruning the very wickedness out of my heart.

Looking back, I'm now thankful for that painful experience
And for the wonderful life with you I now get to experience.

## Dead Weight

You were the misfit in my life
That held me back from all my hopes and dreams.

Like dead weight,
You sank me down to the bottom of the ocean's sea.

I was drowning but didn't know it,
Until burning in my chest prevented me to breathe.

Like the Black Sea, you made my life so murky
That at times it was hard for me to see

Or even think clearly.

And it took me a while to figure out
That you just weren't right for me,

Because you didn't love me.

Not really, when you consider the fact
You kept me under your thumb just so you could control me.

You bent me to your will, and your plan was complete
When you drained the will right out of me.

*L. Marcia Williams*

Now, I can't say that I wasn't warned,
Because I was but chose not to listen.

And now I'm facing the consequences
And repercussions of my lack of judgment.

It took taking a long look at myself in the mirror
Before I realized that who I saw wasn't who I wanted to be.

I had to break away from you for my life's sake,
And yet still it wasn't easy,

Because I had conditioned myself to be with you,
Listen to you and love no one else.

But now that I have my freedom,
I'm picking up the pieces and recreating a whole new self.

## Exposé

The exposé that was done on my life
Didn't cast me in a very good light.

    Bratty, selfish and full of pride
    Was the person I saw through the slides.

It was amazing how much I couldn't see:
The reality of the situation, the reality of me.

    Seeing who I was didn't bring about much pride.
    In fact, it left a hollow feeling inside,

And a new desire to change my ways
After taking responsibility and all the blame.

    But I know that during the next exposé,
    I'll see slides of a person who is not the same.

## Final Notice

This is your final notice from me;
I gotta get away, gotta be free.
And with you that could never be,
So this is your goodbye from me.

I hope you finally find some peace,
The kind that's eluded you and me.
Together we're like a scarlet letter;
All I feel is shame, and I desire better

Than someone like you,
Who made me choose between self-esteem
And treating you like a king,
Between wholeness and living in insecurity.

I foolishly chose you,
And thought you were worthwhile.
Your handsome face
Masked your dubious smile.

By the time I realized it,
It was much too late.
You'd weakened my armor
And sealed my fate.

Your brand of love
Beat me down like the sun.
I saw no one but you,
Not even my own reflection.

But I eventually did,
And didn't like one bit
The kind of girl I allowed to exist.

That is why
This is your final notice from me.
Take it or leave it.
There's no turning back for me.

## Frenemy

I call fake friends like you frenemies.
You're in between a friend and an enemy,

Which means, quite frankly,
I don't trust you.

It doesn't mean
That I won't stop and talk to you.

But it will be about nothing of importance,
And my friendship with you is not important.

You're just an acquaintance that I speak to.
But trust, I know how to keep it moving too,

Right past you as if you don't exist.
If you cross me, you won't be missed.

But remember, I don't count you as an enemy.
Simply put, you're just a frenemy.

## In My Own Skin

I've spent my entire life
Uncomfortable in my own skin,
Weighed down by insecurities
Which slowly killed me within.

I wanted to be smarter, taller,
Thicker, amongst other things,
Not realizing that those things
Wouldn't necessarily bring peace,

Peace that I'd longed for
For so long to materialize,
To fill the gaping hole
I've always felt deep inside.

So, the question is: How do I become
Comfortable in my own skin?
To quench the insatiable need
To garner others' acceptance?

I guess I should start by accepting me,
And all that God created within me,
And not look at them as negatives
But start seeing myself as unique.

*L. Marcia Williams*

Because I'm the only one He created
In this skin to walk this earth.
I may not like everything,
But at that moment He chose me first

To come into this world,
To make a difference with my existence,
For me to realize that I'll be okay
With His assistance.

Being comfortable in my own skin
Means recognizing God's love for me.
He accepts me just as I am
And still loves me unconditionally.

## L-I-F-E

How is life supposed to be?
Will someone please explain it to me?

They say that life should be filled
With purpose and meaning,

That at times you have to press forward
Despite what you're feeling,

Because wallowing in situations
You can't change causes setbacks.

You waste valuable, precious time
That you cant never get back.

That's all well and good,
But I have questions about my innermost,

That little voice inside that says
To trust Him with my heart and soul.

I've heard the owner of that voice
Was God, but I really need to know more.

Does He really have the keys to my life?
Is He able to unlock every door?

Can He answer every question
That I've locked away inside my heart?

Does He really have a plan for me
And for my life a brand new start?

If you're curious about the same things
I've been battling in my inner self,

Will you take the time to ask
The same questions that I just asked myself?

## Life's Blindsides

Fire burns in the center of my chest
As I stare into the face of disappointment.

It seems that dreams really don't come true,
At least if they pertain to getting into your dream school,

Which is something I've worked my entire life to achieve,
So it hurts knowing that they won't accept
The best efforts from me.

My only consolation is that I was accepted by my second
And third choices, which would make anyone else happy
And cause them to have joyful voices.

My parents say that sometimes life just works out that way,
And that I should persevere and try to make the best of things.

Well, if this is part of what I have to look forward to in life,
This experience has prepared me for future blindsides.

## Life's Wars

War is happening everyday
right outside my windowpane,

Not necessarily hand to hand
combat, but war to overcome pain

And other misfortunes
brought on by the trials of life

That we all have to face
and find enough strength to fight.

But they too shall pass,
if we don't lose faith and hope,

And believe that a higher power
won't leave us in a battle zone

All alone and destitute,
waiting on an untimely demise.

He has our lives in His hands
and is our ultimate ally.

## Misunderstood

~ I am a teenager ~
A member of the most
Misunderstood species on the planet.

A gauntlet of emotions flow through me daily,
Whether or not I plan them.

Some good and others bad, but they have
Nothing to do with the type of person I am,

And all to do with the growth process
That I am going through as I learn to control them.

But unfortunately sometimes I'm not afforded
That opportunity and am automatically labeled.

Troublemaker and hard to deal with are just a few
That have already been tossed at me.

I rue the day when teenagers became
So overly judged and misunderstood completely.

## Not Your Fault

Your existence is not a mistake.
It's not your fault that you were the product of rape.

So, you shouldn't try to carry that burden on your shoulders,
A weight so heavy it often feels like a boulder.

It's bogging you down, preventing forward progress.
Nothing allows escape from the pain in your chest,

Because deep down you feel you shouldn't be here,
And your heart bleeds daily, as if struck by a spear.

But I'm here to tell you to let go of what you couldn't control.
Don't let it continue to eat at you and gradually kill your soul.

Although you had no say so in the circumstances of your birth,
I believe you were put here for a perfect purpose on this earth.

## **Purity**

Like Olive Oil, you've remained Extra Virgin,
Even as society has pulled back the curtain

And introduced sex through mainstream media.
Have as much as you like is the main idea,

But you see the benefits of maintaining your purity.
Clear thoughts, focused goals are your securities.

While others fall victim to the pressures of peers,
You've set your own standards that will save many tears.

## S-E-X:
## The 2nd Revelation

You know, this is not the first time
That I have brought about this topic.
A lot of people probably thought
That I would just drop it,

But they can guess again,
'Cause I'm more serious now
Than I have ever been.

There are a lot of you
Who think it's okay to have premarital sex,
But what you don't know
Can get you into a whole lot of mess.

Some still don't believe
There are S.T.D's going around,
And if you're one of them,
You might find yourself six feet in the ground.

Ladies!
I'm trying to make you understand
That you should never
Blindly give yourself up to a man.

Guys!
Don't think that I'm trying to exclude you,
'Cause there are some females who sleep around,
And don't give a second thought about the things they do.

The only thing that I'm trying to say
Is that sex is not something that should be taken lightly.
Some naive people think it's okay,
And others jump in excitedly.

But I'm here to tell you that they're wrong.
I know this might sound like that same old song,
But the truth is you need to know,
And I feel that it's my duty to let you know

That your body is a very sacred thing.
It's worth waiting for the vows and the ring.
Well, that's about as much of this song that I'm going to sing.

Maybe the next time
You think about having premarital sex,
You'll think of all the pain
And heartache that it's destined to bring.

## September 11

September 11 is a day that we won't forget.
It's the day that our country faced a major threat

To liberties and freedoms we all take for granted
By terrorist whose goal was to wipe us off the planet.

What we believe and stand for is what they hate:
Land of the free and home of the brave is what we claim.

Three thousand innocent people died that day,
As our nation mourned and tried to wrap around our brains

That parts of our country were forever marred.
Not one heart in America was left unscarred

On a day on which memories of events were forever engrained
Of fallen heroes and victims that each year we commemorate.

## Skin Tone

We all have our various skin tones
That have nothing to do with the hearts
That we own or the person we are deep down inside,

So we should never judge someone
By the naked eye, which allows us to see colors,
Instead of the hearts of others,
Who may become life long friends,

If we could only see past the color of their skin,
And realize the person they truly are
Outside of the skin in which they were born.

*L. Marcia Williams*

## Tomorrow

Tomorrow is just a day away,
And some take things for granted,
Because they think they'll always
Have another day.

But what they don't know is that,
In reality, they won't always have a tomorrow,
Or that their tomorrow may be filled
With pain and sorrow.

A lot of people put things off
Because they think that they'll have time
To do it tomorrow.

But what they don't know
Is that every second counts,
And that time is very precious to borrow.

Oh, you'll stop skipping school tomorrow,
But today they kicked you out.
Oh, you'll stop texting while driving tomorrow,
But today you were killed in a fatal car crash.

Oh, you'll stop having premarital sex tomorrow,
But today you contracted the H.I.V virus.
Oh, you'll accept Jesus into your heart tomorrow,
But today you died in your sleep.

Look, the only thing that I'm trying to say is:
Stop putting things off until tomorrow;
Get things right today, because tomorrow
Could very well be too late.

## Vice

It was a mistake the day I let you into my life,
The day you gained control, became my vice;
And ever since I've been trying to let go,
Or get you to let go of me,
But it seems I'm far in too deep
For that to be a possibility.
You started off as my enjoyment,
But soon became my employment.
Because I worked hard to have you,
I had to spend more time with you.
Like a fish to a fisher's pole
You had me on your hook.
And believe it or not, once was all it took
For me to crave you insatiably,
To long for you intolerably.
And now I can't sleep without thinking of you
And all the things that we do,
Can't wait to be awake so again I can have you.
Now deep down I know that being with you is wrong,
But I'm just so used to you; we've been together so long.
You've taken over my life.
Nothing else has mattered except my all consuming vice.
My relationships have shattered,
And no one can reach me,
'Cause you're the only one I see.

Or could it be the only one I want to see?
They both mean the same to some degree.
I've allowed you to control me,
Steal precious time away from me.
But this has got to stop.
My life, I need you out,
And I've secretly felt this way for a while,
But getting away from you, I didn't know how.
But now it's clear to me that I must fight,
Do everything I can to get you out of my life,
'Cause you're slowly killing me inside
And that took me a while to realize,
But now I see it with wide eyes,
And to allow you to linger
Would be to my demise.

## Worth

I'm worth more than what meets the eye when you look at me,
Worth more than my bra size, how I fit in my jeans.

I'm worth more than what rappers say in songs about me:
That I should easily let you in between my knees.

I'm worth more than what the media tries to sell to me:
That I should do what just feels right, be free with my body.

I'm worth more than the words you try to lure me with:
That loving you means giving up my most precious gift.

I'm worth more than gaining the title of being your lover,
Worth more than living my life in the minds of others.

I'm worth more than the whispers people say about me.
I see it each time I look down at my promise ring.

# LOVE

## 5 AM Alarm

I was receptive to your charm,
Like a 5 A.M. alarm.
I wanted no parts of you,
But now I've been disarmed
By the feelings you evoke
In me at a moment's notice.
I had no choice in the matter;
You were my heart's focus.
But that doesn't mean
I didn't fight you at every turn.
Learning how to accept defeat
Was a hard lesson to learn.
I felt I wasn't ready for
A relationship so serious,
But it seems my heart
And soul had different ideas.
Now, I can honestly say
I'm glad I lost the war,
And didn't miss out on a rare,
Once in a lifetime love.

*L. Marcia Williams*

## Almost Love

What we had together was almost love;
It was topsy-turvy and gut clenching,
But it wasn't love,

> Just an abbreviated version of it
> That had us as each other's focus.
> But at the end of the day,
> It was more of an infatuation.

Now, the hard part
Was coming to that realization,
Because of the sensations
I felt when you were near.

> But my vision around you was never clear.
> When I finally stepped back for a moment,
> And put everything else into focus,

I realized that what we had wasn't love.
But it was almost there, almost love.

## Assured Love

The first time I saw you,
Your eyes spoke to me,
And ever since,
Our love's been one of reciprocity.

I feel a safety and assurance
That was foreign before.
My heart just wasn't used
To someone like you at its door.

But now our love feels
Like a second skin and nature.
And although it's new, I'm really
Looking forward to our future.

## Best Friend

You're my best friend, and I love you.
There's not much I wouldn't do for you,

And I know with you, the feeling's the same.
And it's been like that ever since the first day.

It was then I knew that we'd be inseparable.
You put up with me even when I'm insufferable,

Which goes well beyond the call of duty.
But the strength of our bond has caused you to
Really know me,

As best friends should know each other.
We could never hold a grudge against one another,

Because the love we share is too deep,
More than a friend and almost like a sibling.

Best friends for life is the label that we share.
You own a piece of my heart that I know
You'll handle with care.

### Catching Feelings

I'm amazed at how hard
and fast I fell for you.

You weren't even my type,
and all of this was so new.

I just know that one day
I looked at you differently.

You smiled at me, and I
immediately began catching feelings,

Feelings that felt like butterflies
fluttering in my stomach,

Feelings so deep that I was afraid
to let you know of them.

But I didn't have to,
because you let me know your feelings.

I found out that I wasn't
the only one catching these feelings.

## Encompassed By Love

When you look into my eyes,
You realize the passion that resides

Deep in the very depths of my soul,
As pure as the sunrise.

It's something I don't try to hide;
In fact, I welcome the consumption

Of feelings that flow freely,
And allow me to function

And live life to the fullest,
Because you're a part of me.

It's a once in a lifetime love
That totally encompasses me.

## Forever Endlessly

When I saw you in the hallway,
I felt my heartbeat accelerate

And go right into overdrive
The moment I looked into your eyes.

Right then, I knew I was a goner
And couldn't stand still any longer.

So, I made a decision and my approach;
Then you looked at me, and we were alone

Inside a world of our own, where time paused.
I felt an unfamiliar feeling within that you caused.

It felt like the first day of the rest of our lives,
Which is funny 'cause I never believed in love at first sight.

But you've made a believer out of me,
And now I plan to love you forever endlessly.

## Guided By Love

It's funny how love comes
when you least expect it.
Falling in love with you
is something I haven't regretted.
Because what we share is as pure
as the morning sunrise.
I get a case of butterflies
with each look into your eyes.
You make me feel warm,
cherished and special inside.
My heart is soaring higher than ever
with love as its guide.

## I Love You

The words "I love you"
should not be taken lightly.
They can build you up
and make you feel strong and mighty.

When you say, "I love you,"
you're connecting with someone's heart.
And if you betray that love,
you risk tearing it apart.

The words "I love you"
mean that you'll always be true.
Through the thick and thin
they can always count on you.

God gives us a special love
to share with a special person.
So, please don't give that love away
if you're not sure and certain.

## I Want To Know

I want to know what love is,
Know how it feels to have a first kiss,

Be able to hold hands in hallways,
Be walked to my car after school days.

I want to share the beat of my heart with another,
To share a special bond with each other,

To have someone who will always have my back.
If my world crumbles, I can fall back on that.

I want to know, and hopefully, I get the chance to know
Someone worthy enough to give my heart to own.

## LOVE

Love, "What is love?"
I ask myself that question as I say this poem.

Is love when your heart nearly skips a beat?
Or is it how you feel after being knocked off your feet?

Is it the thrill in your spine after kissing the first time?
Or is love the way you feel when you look into their eyes?

It seems there are so many definitions of what love might be,
But my definition of love is simply you and me.

## Love At War

>My heart is at love and war with you,
>Because I think I love you too much.
>But when I'm with you, it seems it isn't enough.

The way you make me feel inside
Is overwhelming, downright scary at times.

>And that's what my heart contends with,
>Whether or not I should go down with the ship.

But after weighing both the cons and pros,
It's clear that you're the one my heart chose.

>So, how can I be at war with something
>I don't have control in when my heart
>Has spoken, love has spoken.

## Love Drug

Your love is like a potent drug that keeps me high,
Can't explain what it does to me, or the reason why.

It's the elixir and fixer to all the wrong in my life,
Can't imagine existing without you by my side.

So I don't choose to; it feels good to not have to
Breathe a breath of air without a good dosage of you.

You were the missing piece to this hazy life and my heart,
But now it's complete, nicely filled by your love.

*L. Marcia Williams*

## Love Interest

Your love is like a good investment
that accrues interest.

You've doubled the percentage
you own of my heart.

When you took the time
to learn me and my interests,

That alone made me never
want us to be apart.

I've never felt so well
and thoroughly loved before;

All of my past loves
can't begin to compare.

My heart has never felt
this type of love at its core;

I'm so thankful for the type
of bond that we share.

For you are the one that makes
each day worth living;

My love for you knows no bounds,
because it's infinite.

I'm so honored to share
with you these special feelings.

A future together,
I believe, is completely definite.

## Love Unafraid

When our eyes met,
Baby, I felt our souls connect,
And I know you felt it too
By the way you bit your lip and began to chew.

I know you peeped my swag and my thug appeal,
But ima fall back and keep it real.
Bottom line boo, you was feeling me,
And since I noticed you noticing me,

I felt compelled to let it do what it do,
Make my move and step to you.
And ever since that day,
You've been my shorty, my boo, my babe.

Although a lot of guys get called soft
For talking this way,
The way you make me feel
Makes me unafraid.

## Love Unfamiliar

I never knew things could be this way
between you and me,
that even in a crowded room
you're the only one I can see.
These feelings are so unfamiliar,
but, at the same time, welcome.
I'm so happy when I'm with you
that our time apart is seldom.
I get this spinning, sizzling feeling inside
whenever you're near.
Joy bursts from inside my heart
when it's your voice that I hear.
Your mere presence is so soothing
that at times it melts my soul
right at your feet, solidifying
the greatest love I've ever known.

## Lovely Feelings

I think I fell in love with you
the first time our eyes met.

Though I haven't said the words,
they're implied in my texts.

After each one that I send
with a smiley face at the end,

Lets you know that I want to be
more than just friends.

When we're together,
my whole world feels suspended

By the feelings you fill me with,
and I hope there is no ending

To our story, even in this early chapter
things are beginning to bloom.

And I know I'll be able to speak out loud
how I feel for you real soon.

## Round And Round Game

Just when I thought
my feelings for you were eviscerated,
>> You came along with lines that
>> made things more complicated.
>>> And now we're back in this thing
>>> again, deeper than before.

But pretty soon, I'll be saying
I can't take this anymore.
> It's a round and round game
> we play in a love that won't fade.
>> You've infiltrated my system
>> and just won't go away.

Now, I love to love you,
but sometimes I hate to love you.
> And if I'm honest, there's only
> a thin line separating the two.
>> We can't continue in this
>> seesaw love out of familiarity.

We need to examine to see
if our love can find some solidarity.

## Stunner (Boy Meets Girl)

I was stunned when you walked in my class with a pass
From Guidance, and my heart began to beat fast,

Because I never saw a girl as pretty as you before.
To find out your name, I was ready to put in work;

My cell informed it was twenty minutes 'til the last bell,
As I sat in my seat, palms sweaty, skin turning pale.

I thought of ways to track you down after school,
Hoping you wouldn't see me as some lovesick fool.

But it was a risk that I was just going to have to take,
'Cause you filled me with a feeling I just couldn't shake.

And I didn't want to 'cause the feeling was so brand new,
One that I've gone on to explore after finding you.

## The Way

It's the way that you look at me
When I'm looking at you,

The way you make me feel
When there's no one else, just us two,

The way you smile at me
To let me know that you care,

The way you hold me close
To let me know that you're always there.

But most of all, it's the way
That you treat me and let me be myself,

That lets me know I'm worth
More to you than anyone else.

*L. Marcia Williams*

## The Ways That I Love You

The ways that I love you cannot be counted.
True love seemed elusive, but I finally found it
When I bumped into you that fateful night
And made the best mistake I ever made in life.
Your heart spoke to mine when I looked into your eyes.
From that moment forward, our lives were entwined.
You've become the rain to my earth; you were Heaven sent.
You've proven that true love really does exist.

## When I looked Into Your Eyes

When I looked into your eyes, my spirit froze.
I believe it recognized the other half of its soul.

Through our bodies, I felt a kinetic flow
As I moved toward you like an open door.

My feelings for you were pure from the start.
You walked into my life and entered my heart.

In your eyes, I saw great colors and visions,
And from what I saw, I knew I'd made the right decision

To willingly place my tender heart in your hands,
To recognize that we would be more than just friends.

But most of all, when I looked into your eyes
I found that life had blessed me with a beautiful surprise.

## You Never Knew....

When you walked in the class,
And the professor said your name,
My world stood still,
My heart was never the same.
I wished you had looked my way
And simply noticed me.
I've been waiting since that day
For you to come back to me.
But you were just a messenger,
Passing a pass in my class.
Although I've never seen you again,
For you, I still got it bad.

## Young Love

Your love is like a drug
that inoculates my pain.

It seeps through my system,
right from my veins.

And suddenly,
there is no more hurt or tears.

The very nearness
of you annihilates my fears.

My heart longs for you
to be in my life for always.

I can feel your love for me
even on the worst days.

Some wait a lifetime
for true love to come their way.

So glad I found mine young
and hope that you're here to stay.

## Your Love

When I look into your eyes,
I can see a vision of us clearly,
Knowing that you are the one
I want to be with for eternity.

I know that you're the one
that God has sent for me.
You are everything I ever imagined
a perfect mate would be.

When I look at your face,
I see nothing but grace,
Knowing that in your heart for me,
there will always be a place.

Your love is like a cool breeze
on a hot summer day,
Making me feel good
in its own special way.

You know, I never thought
that this could ever be,
Meeting someone who adores
and loves me unconditionally.

# PAIN

## 4-Get Me Not

Do me a favor and promise
That you'll never forget me.
Treasure and honor me for all of eternity.
I know that you're hurting,
Because you think that you've lost me.
But even though I'm not there physically,
Just check your heart,
And that's where I'll always be.
So, whenever you close your eyes
Just give me a thought, and remember
These words 4-Get Me Not.
Please, do not shed your tears
For me anymore, for God has opened up
To me Heaven's precious door,
A place where there is no more hurt,
Pain or sin; a new start
Where your new life can begin.
So, please, go on living life,
Because that's how it's supposed to be,
If not for yourself, then just do it for me.
And whenever you close your eyes,
Just give me a thought, and remember
These words 4-Get Me Not.

## Alone

I feel so alone in this world.
I have no family to call my own,

So my life is like that of a lost child
Trying to find its way on a long mile.

At night, I cry broken tears of sorrow,
For my heart is filled with the fears of tomorrow.

Will I make it, an abandoned child of sixteen?

There's still so much I don't know and haven't seen.
The emptiness in my heart completely consumes me,

And my life feels devoid of significant meaning.
But I've heard whispers of someone who can provide healing.

We haven't been introduced; I don't know Him personally.

But I wish I did, if He can do all that they say,
Like heal all wounds and chase loneliness away.

I'm willing to place my heart in this Jesus' hands
In exchange for a brand new start and life with Him.

## Betrayal

You betrayed my trust.
I never thought that this would become us,

Facing each other in a place I don't recognize.
The end of our relationship all but finalized.

It's a reality that I could never foresee,
Losing someone I once loved so dearly.

But unfortunately, we can't go back in time,
Undue damage that crossed sacred lines.

So, this is the end of the road, as we once knew it.
Our last chapter, our final conclusion.

## Despise

You don't know the pain that I feel.
It's going to take a long time
For my heart to heal.

But to you my feelings don't seem to be real,
And you seem to think that breaking my heart
Wasn't such a big deal.

Well, you know what?
My heart hurts like hell!
But you act like you can't even tell!

If you looked into my eyes,
You would see the hurt and pain that lies.
And even though I try to put on a disguise,

You would see that it is you I despise.

## Digesting Pain

Sometimes the pain is hard to digest
When your parent says you're less than the best,

Or that you're simply not good enough.
When you thought their job was to build you up,

And not break you down into little pieces,
Say hurtful things then say they don't mean it.

When you know they spoke directly from their heart,
But accepting that is really the hardest part.

Because they helped bring you into this life,
But they tear you down with all their might.

That pain doesn't get any easier to digest,
But you have to move past it and still strive to be the best.

## Hanging Hopes

News stories are rampant about hanging hopes,
Children who just couldn't find a way to cope

    With issues of bullying or discord at home,
  Who decided to cease their lives at the end of a rope—

Lives that never got the chance to reach their potential,
Lives that were celebrated at a premature funeral.

    What can be done to prevent hanging hopes?
  The same thing that gives children courage and hope:

Love and compassion are needed to be spread around
To those who feel that their lives no longer count.

    We are all God's children with purposes in life;
  It's time we share this with others in hopes of saving a life.

## Harsh Realities

All I see are the tracks of my tears
As my makeup messily smears

And runs down my swollen face,
Because today you made me face

The possibility of going our separate ways,
Because apparently you no longer feel the same

As we both did on our first date.
And now it's not me that you choose,
But you say that I'll be better soon.

Because it's not me, it's you, yet that doesn't really matter
When you're leaving me, and my world feels shattered,
And my heart feels battered

With the knowledge it no longer has you to love.
But I guess that's my problem,
Since you've made it no longer yours.

## Heart Scars

I have so many scars on my heart;
Hiding them all is the hardest part.

Constant pain swallows me each day--
I can barely breathe or move a certain way.

Because the hurt seeps through my pores,
Spills down my body and onto the floor,

Which is where my heart is most times,
Trampled by those who only appear to
Love me sometimes.

**High School Pain**

I was born with a defect
that makes me different.

Dealing with kids in high school
has been really hectic.

Those who make fun of me
for something that I can't control

Don't know the damage,
each day, that they're doing to my soul.

Silent tears that I cry
'cause I don't want them to know it.

My hidden face in bathroom stalls
'cause I don't want to show it.

The embarrassment I feel for something
that one in ten thousand are born with

Is hard to deal with at times
and weighs heavily on my mind,

As I wish for a cure for the diagnosis
and the pain on the inside.

My parents taught me to be strong,
but that's easier said than done.

They don't know that this experience
has made high school no fun.

## Hostage

I watched my father
Hold my mother hostage my entire life.
He did it by holding his paycheck to her head,
Instead of a gun or knife.

Now, I'm sure that wasn't what she signed up for
When she became a housewife.
But as a stay-at-home mom
That was the sad tale of her plight.

He threatened to leave her daily,
Penniless without his paycheck.
If she didn't bend to his will,
He'd even decide whether to pay the rent,

The light bill, or any other bills
That were due when he got into one of his moods,
Leaving her scrambling to borrow
From others in order to make it through.

Now certainly, this didn't leave
A good impression on me.
I just know that my heart felt lighter
Whenever I saw him leave.

## Jekyll and Hyde

Jekyll and Hyde was my father,
Which made growing up that much harder.
The inconsistency that he dealt to me
Left a world filled with insecurity.

>At times, I was treated like choice gold,
>Then later, like a thing of old.
>I didn't matter; he could do without me.
>But it was cool, since he provided material things.

Psychologically damaged to the point
I wanted to die.

To escape away from the pain,
I wanted him to die.

>Until I realized that I had a Heavenly Father
>Who wouldn't disappoint me like my earthly father.
>He taught me to trust Him who was in control,
>And gave me hope as the lover of my soul.

I learned to bless those who cursed and mistreated me,
Even if they were the ones responsible for birthing me.

But I forgive you Dad!

## Love Disintegrated

I had a bird's eye view
As I watched our love disintegrate,
A love that was once beautiful
Slowly turned into hate.

Was it our fate to find love
Only to lose ourselves inside of it?
I became more in love with the idea
Of love without even realizing it.

I loved the way others said
How in love we were even when I sensed a change.

I didn't want to acknowledge it,
Because the thought of losing love made me afraid.

Even when it was no longer found
Behind the words that flowed between one another,
I still didn't want to let go of the precious love
I had once discovered.

It was that delusion I finally concluded
That had me trapped inside a loveless love,
When, in reality, the love we'd once shared
Was already long gone.

## My Dear Sweet Aunt (Gwen Muse)

My dear sweet aunt,
Your smile was filled with love
That poured forth from your heart.
You could feel it in your touch,
And taste it in any dish you cooked.

My dear sweet aunt,
You gave of yourself freely
To anyone you saw in need.
You certainly saw the best in me,
And encouraged me to follow my dreams.

My dear sweet aunt,
It's hard to imagine that you're gone,
Something I haven't fully wrapped my head around.
I can still hear your voice's sound
Every time I lay my head down.

My dear sweet aunt,
Pain fills my heart now.
But I know you're part of God's house now.
So, I'll say goodbye for now,
My dear sweet aunt.
With Love ~ L

## My Pen, Pad And I

A tear falls from my eye
With each line that I write.

But a pen and pad are therapeutic;
Words created are rather soothing.

Pulled from the deepest parts of my soul,
They heal old wounds and bandage all hurts
That I may not want to speak out loud.

My pen, pad and I are the only one's allowed
To witness secret love, pain and heartbreak,
My feelings of triumph or mistakes I make.

I'll always cherish the bond between us,
A sure relationship built on secrecy and trust.

## **Night Crimes**

Shouts and screams are all I hear
As I wake up filled with so much fear

That this may be the time he actually hits her,
Physically harms my mom because they differ,

Or whatever it is his mind has created this time
That turns this from a peaceful night
Into one filled with crime.

And if he hits her, I'll call the police
To see if they can come
And bring about some peace,

Or at least take him away
And place my mother out of harms way

Until she can make an important decision
On whether living like this is truly worth it.

## Nightmare On My Street

I took one look into your eyes
as you waved to the movers goodbye.

And when you noticed me from across the street,
all I could do was sigh.

You walked right over and introduced yourself,
and I felt an immediate spark

Between the two of us that was so strong
it could've lit up the sky after dark.

From then, things moved pretty quickly
and soon I was your girlfriend.

It was like a fantasy, but soon became a nightmare
written by Stephen King's pen.

When you said I was yours
and would never belong to any other guy,

I thought it was cute, until the day you twisted
my arm for looking at one passing by.

You grabbed me around my neck
and insisted that I show you some respect.

I was too afraid to even move,
let alone tell anyone what you did.

My parents never suspected a thing,
even when I made excuses for bruises.

I was an athlete and things like that happened;
only I knew that they were ruses.

It all came to a head when one day
a teacher caught you beating me after school.

My parents were called, the police informed
and I was delivered from the nightmare of you.

## One Shot

Dedicated to all the children who died from gun violence~

One shot was all it took to put out a light.
One shot was all it took to steal the apple of an eye.

Innocent children taken by single gunshots;
To steal futures, hopes and dreams was the enemy's plot.

Now loved ones are left to cry sorrowful tears
Thinking of what could've been the brightest of years

For their little ones, who were taken much too soon.
And now their hearts are filled with misery and gloom,

As one shot has forced them to bid their final goodbyes
To a child that was once the center of their lives.

## Pain Extreme

How do you explain your feelings
when the pain is too extreme?

How do you convey the words
when your entire world is hurting?

I can't articulate the way

Your leaving me has left me.
The emptiness inside has made that an impossibility.

I loved you more than I ever thought I could.
Loving you was so easy; our love, like you, was full of good.

The day that you left me, I don't need a calendar date
To remember the pain, the internal, cold, gray rain

That poured out on the inside but did not leak from my eyes,
Because the pain was too extreme, much too much to realize

The finality of the moment,
So, I sat there with my eyes open

When you departed from my life,
And left everything out of focus.

And yet, I'm asked again to explain
The feelings pouring out of me.

Well, how do you explain your feelings
When the pain is too extreme?

L. Marcia Williams

## Painful Lessons

As I looked down at my heart
lying on the floor,
I realized that to you,
I was nothing more

Than someone whose feelings you could abuse,
And that saying that you loved me was just a ruse.

The pain that I felt made me want to run and cover myself
Away from your danger and seek immediate help.

As you looked into my eyes to say you'd met someone new,
Your feelings had changed, but it wasn't me it was you.

How convenient for you to have someone new to love
When there were so many things in my life that I put you above.

I guess I'll just have to chalk this up
to a painful lesson learned:
Putting all your stock into one person
could very well leave you burned.

## Painfully Existing

Silent tears I cry at night,
So tired of this continuous fight

To simply just live my life.
Can anyone else see my plight,

Or understand the pain in my heart?
Because life has really gotten far too hard.

Can I and will I make it?

Are questions that whirl around
In my head every other second.

My doubts, worries and fears suppress me
From living the life that others say I should be.

I guess I just can't see what they see in me:
That I'm talented with a bright future ahead of me.

But I wish I could; it would make things much easier.
Because my heart and soul could sure use a breather.

## Stolen Innocence

You were fifteen years old when you were the victim of rape,
Walking on your way to school when there was a horrible twist of fate.
A masked man grabbed you and stole your innocence away;
He took something that wasn't his and left you to contemplate
Whether living this life was really worth it or truly hopeless,
If a monster could steal your soul and dreams in one single moment.
But you didn't submit to the death that every day you felt inside.
You didn't let it kill you, even though each day was a struggle to fight.
You became a champion for those who were dealt the same crushing blow.
You didn't allow the enemy to defeat you and now offer others a ray of hope.

## The Battle Inside

The dimmed lights in my eyes
Match the soft, silent cries
That only I can hear in my inner ear
As my heart gives in to my inner fears.
Liquid pain hits my pillow each night
As I pray for courage to continue to fight
Negative thoughts that seek to control me,
Take over and slowly destroy me
And keep me from my purpose in life,
Because a dream deferred is a wasted life.
And although the culprit at times is my mind,
I have to win this battle that rages inside.

## Walking Away From Pain

Walking away from pain means walking away from you;
Sometimes it gets hard to separate the two,

Because you are synonymous with the pain that you bring.
You've never made it worth wearing your promise ring,

Because that ring symbolizes the darkness in my life,
A life distraught and filled with so much strife.

High school love is the only thing I used to dream of,
But your cruel words and cold hate have made me weary of

Seeing your face each day when I just want to get away
From the fake smile and false words you say to me each day.

In front of others of course, you have to keep up your game
That shows you love me, but I know your real hate.

You never loved me, and there's been nothing gained.
So, I'm finally walking away from you and all your pain.

## YOU KNOW WHAT!

You know what?

I'm tired of you and your mess.
You're the reason I'm under so much stress.

And you know what?

I don't know why I got with you in the first place;
I should've never looked your way in the first case.

And you know what?

You were never any good for me;
I realize that now and wonder why
I thought that we could ever be.

And you know what?

Well, by now you should know what to expect:
I don't ever want to see you again,
And I sure as hell don't want you back.

## You Said That You Loved Me

You said that you loved me.

You said that you would love and
Honor me for all of eternity.

You said that you loved me.

Why, why did you lie to me?
This is not how love is supposed to be!

You said that you loved me.

But you're not supposed to degrade me
And make me feel like dirt.
When I look back on our entire relationship,
I see that it was based on nothing but lies
And ended in hurt.

You said that you loved me.

So you treated me like I was worthless
And told me that no one else would love me.

And yet, you said that you loved me.

# HOPE

## A Friend

A friend is someone
who is not afraid to lend an ear,

Someone who will help you
through your greatest fear.

A friend will be there
when you're in trouble

And is someone who will
stand up for you and be humble.

A friend is someone
who will always forgive you,

But the reason that they do
is because a friend is true.

## Beauty

It's often said that beauty
is more than skin deep,
And that is true no
matter what people believe.

Because the person you are
comes from within,
And not from the complexion
or attractiveness of skin.

Inward ugliness cannot be repaired
by a surgeon's knife.
But beautifying the insides
 can greatly affect one's life,

And the lives of those
around them in positive ways.
A kind heart can overcome
the most troublesome days.

So, we should work on ourselves
from the inside out,
And allow the world to see
what true beauty is all about.

## **Behind Closed Eyelids**

Behind closed eyelids
I have dreams and visions
Of a future brighter than
I ever could imagine.

So bright is this place
Where I can't be contained.
There are no dream killers
Or unwanted pictures
Of me living short of my destiny.

Folks say they want the best for me,
So I sift purposefully to see
The truth in their eyes, 'cause to my surprise,
Everyone doesn't want the best for you,
And everyone doesn't wish success for you.

But the bottom line is it all falls back to me,
And whether I have enough faith to believe
That through the Creator I can do all things,
And that there is nothing that I can't achieve.

## BFF's

I can look in your eyes
and see what no one else can see:

It's not their fault;
that's just how much in you I believe.

You can do and have anything
you want out of this life,

And I'm here to push you
and stand right by your side.

Through the thick and thin,
I'll be there, so don't worry.

Your struggles will not be the end
or tell the whole story.

I can say all of this
because I know you feel the same for me.

Close as blood, thicker than water,
BFF's is what we'll always be.

## **Bright Future**

My future is bright.
I can see the sunlight
Flashing through positive years
As love fills my heart even when I shed tears.

With knowledge that things
Will eventually work out fine,
I will not be sorrowful,
But relish every second of my earth time.

I will find out everything
The Creator of Life has for me,
And use the Key He has provided
To unlock my destiny.

What God has for me,
No one will be able to take away from me.
My bright future allows me to live
In perfect peace.

## Changed Ways

Some people don't believe
That you can have changed ways,
And that a period in your life
Is sometimes just a phase,

                        Something you're walking through
                           While trying to figure out you.
                        They won't let you forget the past
                          Once you finally realize truth.

But you can't live your life
According to what others think of you.
They didn't die so you could live,
Or bare that cross for you,

                        Weren't there at your lowest point
                          When you cried out for help,
                        Weren't there when your very soul
                            Was delivered from hell.

So, how can they make the claim
That you can't have changed ways,
When the proof is in the pudding,
And you know you're not the same?

## Glue

You are the glue
that holds me together;
You stick by me through
the stormiest weather.

Even in my own fault,
you never pull away.
You understand that I'm
human yet love me the same.

You encourage and give me hope
when I don't believe,
let me know that I can count on you
in my time of need.

I've never met a more
consistent person before,
a friend who holds their own
but won't ever let me go.

## Herstory

Herstory comes in a million variations.
She could one day be the leader of our nation,

Or teach the ones that will change our tomorrows,
Or find the solution to end all our sorrows.

Herstory changes from each day-to-day,
And we see different origins in a different face.

Some stories are sad but to others familiar.
They help us understand who she is better.

Herstory is important to each and every one of us;
She bore the man who said, "In God We Trust."

Because of her, men and women make forward progress;
History books are still being written about her success.

## Hope For A Nation

Some people are resistant to change.
They'd rather be stuck in their old ways,

Instead of saying goodbye to olden days
That pushed inequality because of race.

In order to have hope for future generations,
We have to stand together linked as one nation

Under God, indivisible with liberty and justice,
Knowing that if we don't, we won't get to see this

Nation moved forward and flourish as it should.
If closed-minded people would open minds, then we could

Have better days and a better climate to thrive in,
Instead of discord amongst ourselves barely surviving.

## Hopeful Desire

Every thing has to come to an end,
so I'm hopeful that this situation will bend

And eventually move in the right direction.
The hurt and pain will be a reflection

That I can look back on as a battle conquered
of dark, gray days that will exist no longer.

I'm hopeful because this is what I desire and
believing in something is really half the battle.

## Hopelessness (Don't Give In)

Hopelessness is where hope falls apart;
It destroys the spirit and mangles the heart.

So the key is to never become hopeless,
Even when it feels like your life is out of focus,

And you can't find the correct aperture settings,
In life you have to take the bad with the blessings

That are sure to come your way with each breath that you take,
But please don't let it be the death

Of the core of who you are, even when you're uncertain,
Or you feel exposed like a pulled back curtain.

Those feelings will change like the times and seasons,
And you'll better understand life's rhymes and reasons.

## It's Not Over!

It's been spinning in your mind
that your life is over, and you don't think
you can make it in this world much longer.
But you know what?

You can, because you have a purpose
That is solely yours and for which you were chosen

Specifically for as part
of your earth plan.
So, your struggles right now,
you will later understand

If you fight the good fight and believe you can conquer
Whatever life throws at you because you're a warrior

Who was born to succeed
in this complex life,
That was bound to give
an unpleasant surprise.

But you can make it and in the end come out much stronger;
As long as you have breath, IT'S NOT OVER!

## King

This month we celebrate the birth of Martin Luther King,
A man who fought for the equality of all human beings.

Many of his dreams were realized after he was taken away,
Which shows to the world that he didn't fight or die in vain.

Since that fateful afternoon in Memphis, Tennessee,
America has gone on to realize many of his dreams.

No longer do laws push separate and unequal practices.
No longer do black and white entrances and exits exist.

No longer can a person be denied an education based
On the color of their skin; black and white people walk
Hand in hand and become the best of friends.

The sit-ins, marches, boycotts, lynchings, and beatings
All tell the story of a man, who although never got to witness
The first black president, we still think of as King.

*L. Marcia Williams*

## My Hope For You

My hope for you is that you find
Out who you are inside,
That you find the love within
That will take you through life,

That you make decisions
Based on the character built
Through trials and tribulations
And early lessons instilled,

That you see all the beautiful colors
That life has to offer,
And not be jaded
By one experience or another.

'Cause it's guaranteed that some days
Will be harder than others,
And there will be times
When you will feel like you suffer.

But my hope for you is that you know
That you are an overcomer
Of circumstances brought by chance
Or even botched plans,

That you never feel like you're in limbo
Or standing in quicksand,
That you know that I'll always be there
Whenever you need me to lend a hand.

*L. Marcia Williams*

## My One Hope

As dissension falls like raindrops around me,
And light from the stars diminish so vastly,

I look to you this dark hour to guide me
And lead me back to the land of the living.

The thud in my chest is almost at a standstill;
My heart barely beats because it's so pain-filled.

I turn to you, as I am far past my wits end
On what to do; my very soul needs to mend.

You are the last thread of hope that I can call upon
Whose strength in the past from which I have drawn.

So, I'm seeking you today as a source like the sun
To shine on the darkness my world has become.

## Over-Exposed

I see you hurting in your soul;
Pain so raw it's over-exposed.

So, you've decided to shut everyone out
As you try to figure your very life out.

So tired of feeling all alone in this world,
Where everywhere you turn
There's more and more hurt.

People that you trusted have let you down;
Relationships you had are no longer around.

But there's someone who loves and understands you.
He's the only salve for your over-exposed wounds.

So, call on Jesus and accept Him into your heart.
He'll see you through your troubles
And provide a brand new start.

## Overcoming Challenges

Trying to figure life out can be a challenge,
But it's one that I am willing to accept.

The dips and valleys may knock me off balance,
But I have to believe that I am not inept.

I am equipped to overcome any obstacle:
My destiny no enemy will intercept.

I believe and know that all things are possible.
The faith that I have will not leave me bereft.

## Ride Or Die

Emotions surge through my insides
As I try to navigate the roads of this life.

    My mind is going eighty-five on the highway
        Just to get me through to the next day.

But as I look at you sitting on the passenger side,
Watching my back, protecting my blindside,

    I see that I'm truly blessed to have a ride or die friend,
    Someone who will be there when the ride decides to end.

You're right there with me enduring life's speed bumps,
Helping me to avoid crashes, catastrophes and such.

    I want to let you know how much I appreciate you
    For not letting a day go by that I can't count on you.

*L. Marcia Williams*

## Thank You

When pain filled my heart,
You brought hope and a brand new start.

I'll never forget the day you came into my life;
Through a cloud of darkness, you were a welcome light.

And ever since, you've been walking right beside me,
Directing my path, steadily guiding me.

Now, instead of pain, I have the joy and peace
I'd sought for so long to comfort me.

So, I guess I just want to say thank you
For changing my life and making it anew.

## The Beauty of Your Soul

The beauty of your soul gives me hope
That one day I'll finally be able to cope

With the ugliness that this world displays,
Which points to a society lost in disarray.

But I am encouraged by the inner glow
That illuminates your eyes right from your soul.

It touches all who are blessed to surround you,
As you look at the world from a different point of view.

Negativity isn't a focal point you dwell on,
As you approach life with a purpose and reason.

Whatever comes your way, you take in stride,
And never take opportunities to shrink and hide.

In fact, your soul reflects that of a warrior
Soldiering tribulations and coming out superior.

These are qualities that I'll look to as a guide.
The beauty of your soul inspires me to lead a better life.

*L. Marcia Williams*

## The Gift of True Friendship

The repetitive thoughts in my head
Were filled with vibrations that led to dread.

But you wouldn't allow me to stay in that space;
You told me that there would be a brighter day.

And sure enough things eventually got better,
Because nothing can stay the same forever.

You helped me see that and not lose hope,
Even when the darkest days were killing my soul.

When thoughts were rampant about leaving earth,
You helped me see that I had much to live for.

I love you for that, and will always remember
Your heartfelt actions and gift of true friendship.

## Thousands Of Tears

Thousands of tears have stained my face;
Many times it was hard to keep my faith

And believe that things would work out for me
As turmoil took hold so dominantly.

But I held on through the trying times
And didn't let dark clouds destroy my silver line.

Then one day I was able to see through the sunshine.
After my tears dried, I made out just fine.

## Uncertainty

There's so much uncertainty in my life,
But I have to believe things will turn out all right.

The challenges facing me are for a reason.
Like spring and summer, there will be a new season.

The winter blast of troubles that surround me
Will dissipate like fall leaves and blow right past me,

And the sun will shine again so that I can see clearly.
No longer will I be afraid or filled with uncertainty.

## Undisguised

Tears stream down my cheeks
As I pray to God for some peace

    In this broken little life of mine
    That I see fading, starting to decline.

        As I fall on my knees and cry my heart out,
        A space that is filled with so much doubt,

            I feel something shift deep inside
            The hole I've valiantly tried to hide.

    But He sees the real me undisguised.
    All I have to do now is swallow my pride

And acknowledge His presence in my life.
He's promised to never leave my side.

## With My Eyes Open Wide

With my eyes open wide,
I walk through life with nothing to hide,
Jumping at opportunities,
Not letting them pass me by.

With my eyes open wide,
I hold nothing but love in my heart,
Knowing that there's a possibility
That it will get torn apart.

With my eyes open wide,
I see people through their actions,
Always looking closely for their reactions.

With my eyes open wide,
I'm always looking for possibilities,
Never underestimating my capabilities,
Always looking for originality,
Always looking to bring forth unity.

And do you know why?
Because I have my eyes open wide.

## About the Author

L. Marcia Williams is a native of Tampa, FL. She obtained a Bachelor of Arts in English/Creative Writing and a Master of Arts in Library & Information Science from the University of South Florida. She resides in Valrico, FL.

www.ingramcontent.com/pod-product-compliance
Lightning Source LLC
Chambersburg PA
CBHW071701040426
42446CB00011B/1866